P9-DYP-707

TRUE or FALSE?

This slimy-looking thing is neither a plant nor an animal.

TRUE!

It's a fungus. Fungi—there are more than 100,000 species—are their own special group.

How can scientists tell fungi are not plants? Simple. Fungi don't have chlorophyll. That's the stuff plants use to absorb sunlight and make their own food.

And how can they tell fungi aren't animals? Because fungi don't eat and digest food. They simply absorb it as they grow.

Book design Red Herring Design/NYC

Library of Congress Cataloging-in-Publication Data
DiConsiglio, John.
There's a fungus among us! : true stories of killer molds / by John DiConsiglio.
p. cm. — (24/7: science behind the scenes)
Includes bibliographical references and index.
ISBN-13: 978-0-531-12071-2 (lib. bdg.)   978-0-531-17530-9 (pbk.)
ISBN-10: 0-531-12071-6 (lib. bdg.)   0-531-17530-8 (pbk.)
1. Bacterial diseases—Juvenile literature. I. Title.
RC115.D53 2007
616.9'2—dc22   2006006811

THERE'S A FUNGUS

AMONG US

True Stories of Killer Molds

John DiConsilgio

WARNING: You might be thinking, How could a little fungus possibly hurt people? Could it give them bad breath? Athlete's foot? Think again. Fungi can cause bleeding lungs. Brain damage. And more.

Franklin Watts
An Imprint of Scholastic Inc.
New York • Toronto • London • Auckland • Sydney
Mexico City • New Delhi • Hong Kong
Danbury, Connecticut

CONTENTS

Is a mold attacking children in Ohio?

These cases are 100% real. Find out how fungus fighters solved three deadly mysteries.

15 Case #1:
Beware of the Killer Mold!
In Cleveland, Ohio, children are falling sick with a strange lung disease. Is it a toxic fungus?

Case #2:
The Mystery of the Dirt Devil
25 A deadly fungus is hiding in the Southwestern soil. Can Dr. Richard Hector unearth its secrets?

Scientists dig up something deadly in Utah.

35 Case #3:
The Case of the Deadly Tree Fungus
How did a killer fungus travel the globe? And can a scientist find it—before it kills again?

Is a peaceful island in Canada home to a killer?

5

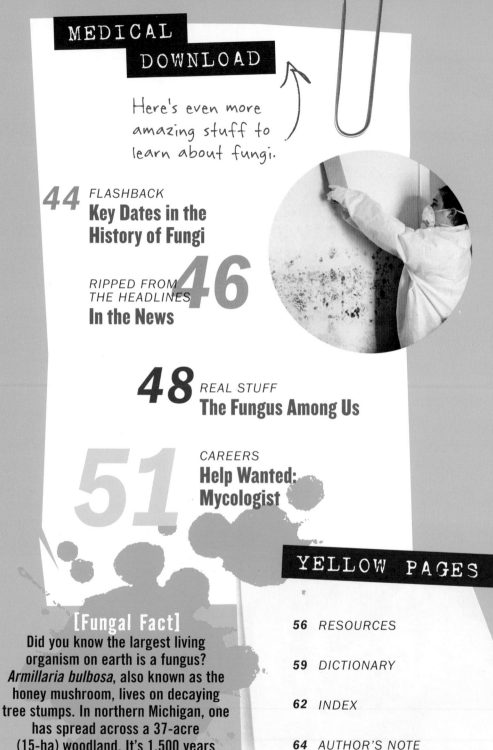

MEDICAL DOWNLOAD

Here's even more amazing stuff to learn about fungi.

[Fungal Fact]

Did you know the largest living organism on earth is a fungus? *Armillaria bulbosa*, also known as the honey mushroom, lives on decaying tree stumps. In northern Michigan, one has spread across a 37-acre (15-ha) woodland. It's 1,500 years old and weighs more than 21,000 pounds (9,525 kg)!

Did you know there are more than 100,000 species of fungi? They can be found anywhere—in the woods, in your basement, even living in your body.

MEDICAL 411

Some fungi, like mushrooms, can be good to eat. But others can make you sick—or even kill you. That's where fungus fighters come in. They figure out what's mold—and what's *killer mold*.

IN THIS SECTION:

▶ how fungus experts really talk;

▶ how fungi can invade your body;

▶ and people who work to fight fungi.

What's the Word?

Scientists who study fungi have their own way of speaking. Find out what their vocabulary means.

I'm the senior **mycologist**. So, I obviously know a disease caused by a **fungus** when I see it.

mycologist
(mye-KOL-uh-jist) a scientist who studies fungi

fungus
(FUHN-guhss) a living thing that is not a plant or an animal

"Myco" means "fungi."

"Ologist" is "someone who studies."

I think the children got sick from **mold**. We'll probably find it in their homes.

mold
(mold) a fungus that grows in damp, dark places and feeds on moisture. It can produce allergy-like symptoms that can be fatal.

Say What?

We investigated, and we found a lot of **spores** in the kids' basements.

spores
(sporz) the seeds that some fungi release into the air. Breathing them can be dangerous.

I'm afraid this type of fungus is highly **toxic**.

toxic
(TOK-sik) poisonous

Here's some other lingo mycologists might use on the job.

contagious
(kuhn-TAY-juhss) describing something, like an illness, that can be spread from person to person by contact
*"Be careful. That's a **contagious** disease."*

prognosis
(prog-NOH-suhss) a prediction about a patient's recovery from an illness
*"The **prognosis** for Mr. Jefferson is good—as long as he takes his medicine every day."*

symptoms
(SIMP-tuhmz) the noticeable signs of a disease
*"The **symptoms** include an itchy, swollen red patch of skin."*

thrive
(thrive) to do well and flourish
*"This **fungus** seems to thrive in warm, dry areas."*

Fungi Gone Wild!

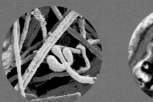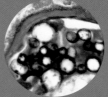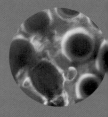

Here's a look at some dangerous fungi—and the damage they can do.

Stachybotrys or stachy, or "toxic mold," for short

symptoms	how you get it	treatment	prognosis
Coughing, sneezing, runny nose, headaches, skin rash, burning eyes, fatigue, and asthma attacks. Stachy can even cause your lungs to bleed.	Stachy lives in damp places. When pipes leak, it grows on wet wood or wallpaper. Stachy releases toxic spores that can be inhaled into your lungs.	Most symptoms will end if you get far away from the mold! Some severe stachy victims may need lung treatments or surgery.	Your chances of recovery are good if you remove the stachy from your home.

Coccidioides immitis or cocci to its friends

symptoms	how you get it	treatment	prognosis
Cocci spores cause 150,000 cases of **valley fever** every year. Breathing problems or painful red rashes afflict 40 percent of infected people. Others have no symptoms at all.	Cocci grows in the soil of the American Southwest. Digging into the ground— or driving across it— loosens toxic spores that drift into your lungs.	Valley fever doesn't generally require treatment. Doctors fight severe cases with anti-fungal drugs.	It usually goes away in six weeks. But one in 200 victims has serious problems, like holes in their lungs. They can also get cocci **meningitis**, a serious infection of the brain.

Cryptococcus or crypto for short

symptoms	how you get it	treatment	prognosis
Exposure to this fungus often triggers allergy symptoms. But it can also cause a rare fungal disease that makes your brain swell.	Crypto usually lives in trees and soil in warm countries like Brazil— although it's even been found in ice-cold Canada. You get sick by breathing in its spores.	Most cases of crypto poisoning require no treatment. As with cocci, doctors use anti-fungal drugs to fight severe **outbreaks**.	It depends. Some victims heal without treatment.

The Medical Team

Scientists work as part of a team. Here's a look at some of the experts who help identify and fight fungi.

BIOLOGISTS
They're scientists who study living organisms. Some specialize in plants or humans. Mycologists are biologists who specialize in fungi.

MYCOLOGISTS
They're scientists who study fungi. They go wherever fungi live—in nature, in homes, in the laboratory, even in books in the library.

INTERNAL MEDICINE DOCTORS
They are usually the first doctors patients see. They can identify problems and call in other specialists.

GEOLOGISTS
They're scientists who study the earth. They play an important role in uncovering fungi that grow in the ground.

ALLERGISTS
They're experts at treating patients who have allergies, including those caused by mold and other fungi.

INFECTIOUS DISEASE SPECIALISTS
They're like medical detectives. These physicians examine blood samples, x-rays, and other lab tests to figure out complicated illnesses.

ENVIRONMENTAL HYGIENISTS
They're scientists who study fungi and other organisms found in human environments, like homes, schools, and workplaces. They diagnose a fungus, and then advise people how to get rid of it.

TRUE-LIFE CASE FILES!

24 hours a day, 7 days a week, 365 days a year, scientists fight fungi that cause illness and death.

IN THIS SECTION:

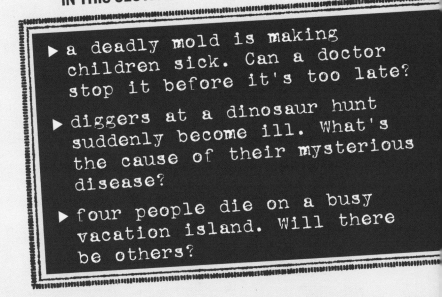

▶ a deadly mold is making children sick. Can a doctor stop it before it's too late?

▶ diggers at a dinosaur hunt suddenly become ill. What's the cause of their mysterious disease?

▶ four people die on a busy vacation island. Will there be others?

How do mycologists get the job done?

Each of the cases you're about to read is very different. But the steps the scientists followed are similar. Fungus experts use a scientific process to figure out which fungi have made patients sick—and what the best treatments are. You can follow this process as you read the case studies. Keep an eye out for the icons below.

THE QUESTION At the beginning of each case, the scientists ask **one or two main questions** they need to answer.

THE EVIDENCE The next step is to **gather and analyze evidence**. They look for symptoms. They run tests. Then they analyze the evidence to figure out what it means.

THE CONCLUSION Along the way, scientists come up with theories about what may have happened. They test these theories against the evidence. **Does the evidence back up the theory?** If so, they've reached a conclusion.

Beware of the Killer Mold!

In Cleveland, Ohio, children are falling sick with a strange lung disease. Is it a toxic fungus?

Mystery Illness

A rare lung disease hits Cleveland's kids. Dr. Dearborn wants to know what's causing it.

It's always hectic in the emergency room. And this Thursday in November 1994 was no different. Dr. Dorr Dearborn was working his usual shift at Cleveland's Rainbow Babies and Children's Hospital. Dearborn is a pediatrician, a children's doctor. He sees sick kids every day.

But one child really troubled Dearborn. He was a six-week-old boy with a bad nosebleed. The doctor quickly realized that the boy's lungs were filling with blood. He had a deadly condition called **pulmonary hemosiderosis**.

That news was bad—and it was about to get worse. The boy was the third child with bleeding lungs that Dearborn had seen that morning.

Pulmonary hemosiderosis is rare. It strikes only one in a million children. The Cleveland hospital sees just two or three cases every ten years.

Dr. Dorr Dearborn works at the pediatric environmental clinic in Cleveland. He studies the effects of outside factors in the environment on children.

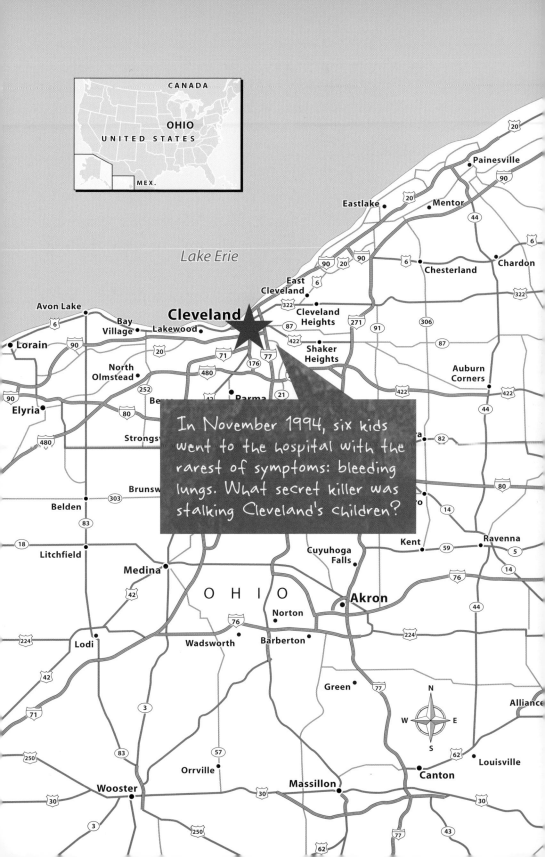

CANADA

OHIO

UNITED STATES

MEX.

Lake Erie

Painesville

20

90

Eastlake 20 Mentor

44

6

Chesterland Chardon

322

90 20 90 6

East Cleveland 6

Cleveland ★

322 Cleveland Heights

271 91 306

87

Shaker Heights

422

Auburn Corners

Avon Lake

6

Bay Village Lakewood

87

71 77

176

Lorain

90

20

North Olmstead

480

252

422

422

44

Elyria

90

80

Be...

42

Parma

21

In November 1994, six kids went to the hospital with the rarest of symptoms: bleeding lungs. What secret killer was stalking Cleveland's children?

82

80

Strongsv...

Brunsw...

303

14

Belden

83

Kent 59 Ravenna

18

Cuyuhoga Falls

5

Litchfield

14

Medina

76

Norton

Akron

44

42

Lodi

76

224

224

Wadsworth Barberton

O H I O

Green 77

N

W E

S

71

Alliance

250

83

57

Orrville

62 Louisville

Wooster

3

30

250

30

Massillon

Canton

30

3

250

77 43

62

Now they had five cases of the little-seen disease. And the day had just started. Dearborn was baffled. "If we see one more," he told another doctor, "we are calling for help."

They didn't have to wait long. Less than 24 hours later, another child was wheeled into the hospital with bleeding lungs.

The message was clear: An unknown killer was attacking Cleveland's children. But what was it? Dearborn needed to find out—and stop it before any kids died!

Examining the Evidence

Dearborn calls in the experts. What clues do they have so far?

To fight the mystery of the kids' bleeding lungs, Dearborn needed help. He called the **CDC**. That's the government agency that investigates outbreaks—everything from bird flu to mad cow disease.

It was after business hours, so he left a

message with a janitor. At 7:30 the next morning, a top CDC investigator returned his call. Within 36 hours, agency leaders arrived in Cleveland. Everyone knew this was serious business.

Dearborn and the CDC team reviewed the facts of the case. What, they asked, did these children have in common? For one thing, they all lived in a poor section of East Cleveland.

That made Dearborn think the cause was an environmental illness. There was something outside their bodies—maybe in their homes or in their schools—that was making these kids sick.

Dearborn and the investigators were racing the clock. They were facing a killer that could be infecting more children by the minute.

When there's serious risk of contagion, workers from the CDC wear protective suits such as this one. The CDC is a government agency. Among their many duties, they work to prevent and control infectious and chronic diseases.

WHAT IS A FUNGUS?

Some taste good on pizza. Others help make bread rise. Why do still others turn deadly?

Fungi have been around for a long time: 900 million years. They are **yeasts**, molds, mushrooms, and **mildews**. And they play an important role in keeping the earth clean because of their unusual eating habits.

Fungi are different from plants. Plants make their own food, using chlorophyll, sunlight, water, and carbon dioxide.

But fungi don't have chlorophyll. They "eat" by absorbing organic matter, like wilted plants and dead trees.

Harmless or Harmful?

Most fungi are harmless. They can even be helpful. Yeasts are used to make everything from bread to beer.

And who hasn't had mushrooms on their pizza? But some fungi are destructive. Instead of eating dead organisms, they eat living things. These fungi create problems—for both plants and people.

One such fungus started the Irish potato famine in the 1840s. It destroyed so many potato plants that a million people died of hunger.

Fungi can also infect people. Some release spores—or seeds—into the air. Breathing them can cause lots of illnesses, from irritating **allergies** to serious lung infections.

Above: Fungi on a pizza. *Top:* Fungi on the leaves of a potato plant.

Solving the Mystery

**The investigators search the victims' homes—
and find what they're looking for!**

The team began their investigation. The first step in finding the potential killer was to interview the sick children's parents.

Dearborn and the CDC investigators asked about anything that might have made their kids ill: laundry detergent, food, and bathroom cleaners. Nothing seemed to fit.

Next, the team searched the families' homes.

They went to 30 homes in one week. They were prepared to climb through ceilings and pull up floorboards. But as soon as Dearborn stepped into the first house, he knew he'd found the problem.

He smelled it in the air. He saw it in the puffy black stains on the ceiling and wallpaper. He noticed it dripping from exposed pipes.

"I didn't need a lot of equipment to find it," Dearborn says. "All I needed were my eyes and my nose."

It was black. It was slimy.

It was killer mold!

The black stains on this wood are killer mold. Dr. Dearborn found stains like these in the homes of the sick children.

21

STACHYBOTRYS—THE KILLER MOLD!

It's black. It's slimy. And it can make you really sick.

Molds are a microscopic type of fungi that occur naturally in our environment. Molds like wet places, and grow easily around leaky pipes, shower curtains, and other damp places in the house.

Most molds are relatively harmless. They can cause mild cold-like symptoms: sneezing, runny nose, headaches, and red, burning eyes.

Toxic Mold

But a type of mold called stachybotrys—or stachy, for short—is different. It's one of a small number of deadly molds. In fact, it's so dangerous that scientists call it toxic mold.

Stachy releases sticky spores that attach to people's lungs. Once inside you, stachy dissolves and spreads a poison called **mycotoxin**.

Bleeding Lungs

Everyone reacts differently to this poison. Some people never know they have it. Others get a bad cough. Still others develop severe infections, like bleeding lungs. Children are at a greater risk of illness from stachy because their lungs are not fully developed.

Doctors can often treat stachy victims with anti-fungal drugs. In severe cases, patients may need lung surgery.

Jeffrey May, a home inspector and mold expert, in his lab in Cambridge, Massachusetts. On the computer screen at left is an enlargement of the mold *Stachybotrys chartarum*.

Identifying the Killer

How did lethal amounts of stachybotrys invade Cleveland?

Dearborn and the CDC team tested the black mold. Sure enough, their worst fear came true: It was stachybotrys ("stachy," for short), a deadly form of mold.

Dearborn wondered, How did so much toxic mold get in the sick kids' homes?

It turned out, the Cleveland kids were in the middle of a stachy-breeding coincidence.

Three months earlier, a huge rainstorm flooded much of Cleveland. The sewers overflowed the city's east side. That produced the perfect conditions for mold growth.

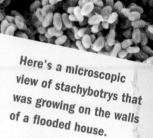

Here's a microscopic view of stachybotrys that was growing on the walls of a flooded house.

The mold attached itself to damp wallpaper and wood in the children's bedrooms. As they slept, their lungs filled with deadly spores.

"It's one thing to have stachy growing in the ceiling of your bathroom. Then you're exposed to it for maybe half an hour a day," Dearborn says. "It's much different if you have it in the wall next to your bed. You are sleeping right next to it for six or eight hours every night."

The Aftermath

Dr. Dearborn lost five young patients to illness—and still battles the dreaded stachy.

Over the next ten years, Dearborn cared for 38 infants with mold-related illnesses. Five of them died.

Many families removed the toxic mold from their homes. Other houses were so covered in stachy that the only solution was to tear them down.

Not every doctor agrees with Dearborn's diagnosis. Some say that stachy is clearly dangerous, but it's not powerful enough to cause the lethal lung disease that afflicts Cleveland's kids.

It's true there's no proven scientific link between toxic mold and illnesses. But some scientists, like Dearborn, say they've seen enough proof in their patients to justify their beliefs.

Today, Dearborn teaches people how to keep their homes safe from mold. He doesn't see a lot of stachy. It's still relatively rare in most houses.

Still, there's no reason to take chances, Dearborn says. If you can see it or smell it, get rid of it! 24/7

Dr. Dearborn discovered deadly mold in people's houses. But how do you unearth a killer fungus that hides in the ground?

The Mystery of the Dirt Devil

A deadly fungus is hiding in the Southwestern soil. Can Dr. Richard Hector and his team of scientists unearth its secrets?

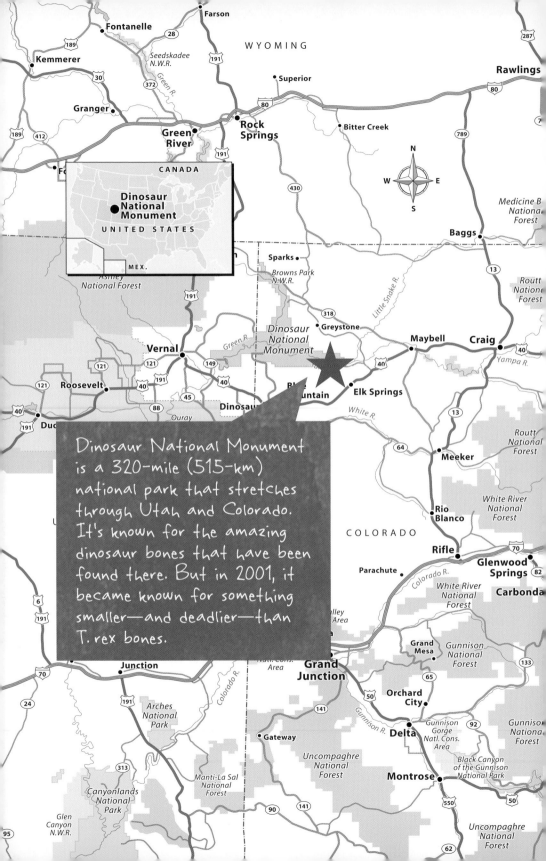

Farson

Fontanelle · 28

189 · **Kemmerer**

W Y O M I N G

287

30 191

Green River
N.W.R.

Seedskadee
N.W.R.

Granger ·

· **Superior**

80

Rawlings

80

372

189 412

Green River

Rock Springs

· **Bitter Creek**

789

191

N
W   E
S

430

Medicine B
Nationa
Forest

CANADA

**Dinosaur
National
Monument**

U N I T E D   S T A T E S

MEX.

Baggs

Ashley
National Forest

191

· **Sparks**

Browns Park
N.W.R.

Little Snake R.

13

Routt
Nation
Forest

318

· **Greystone**

Maybell ·

Craig

40

Vernal

121

121

149

Green R.

Dinosaur
National
Monument

Yampa R.

121

Roosevelt

40 191

40

untain

· **Elk Springs**

40

13

40

88

45

Dinosau

Ouray

White R.

64

Routt
National
Forest

40

Du

191

Meeker ·

White River
National
Forest

Rio
Blanco ·

> Dinosaur National Monument
> is a 320-mile (515-km)
> national park that stretches
> through Utah and Colorado.
> It's known for the amazing
> dinosaur bones that have been
> found there. But in 2001, it
> became known for something
> smaller—and deadlier—than
> T. rex bones.

C O L O R A D O

Rifle ·

70

**Glenwood
Springs**

82

Parachute ·

White River
National
Forest

Carbonda

Colorado R.

6
191

lley
Area

**Grand
Mesa** ·

Gunnison
National
Forest

133

Junction

Natl. Cons.
Area

**Grand
Junction**

65

**Orchard
City** ·

Gunniso
Nationa
Forest

70

Colorado R.

50

141

92

24

191

Arches
National
Park

Gunnison R.

Delta

Gunnison
Gorge
Natl. Cons.
Area

313

· **Gateway**

Uncompaghre
National
Forest

Black Canyon
of the Gunnison
National Park

Manti-La Sal
National
Forest

Montrose ·

Canyonlands
National
Park

90

141

550

50

Glen
Canyon
N.W.R.

Uncompaghre
National
Forest

95

62

The Diggers Get Sick

A team of archeologists and students fall ill after a dinosaur dig in Utah. But why?

In 2001, a team of diggers arrived in Dinosaur National Monument. The group was made up of young **archaeologists** and students.

Their mission was to find out about ancient people who had lived in the area. Archaeologists learn about the past by digging up old buildings and objects. Armed with shovels, picks, and sifters, these diggers pored through the dirt, looking for ancient objects.

Instead, ten of these unlucky diggers found something they didn't expect. After returning home, they fell ill. Some had high fevers, painful red rashes, and severe breathing problems.

There was something dangerous in the dirt of Dinosaur National Monument. And it had infected the diggers.

But what was it, exactly?

Doctors examined the infected archaeologists and students. The team was suffering from a life-threatening disease called valley fever.

Valley fever doesn't affect everyone. But in a small number of cases, it attacks the lungs, brain, bones, and skin. Here a victim shows scars from his battle with valley fever.

VALLEY FEVER AND COCCI

Breathe a few spores of cocci, and you can end up with a terrible disease.

Valley fever can be a painful, lifelong illness. Some patients develop lung cavities—holes—in their lungs. These cavities can only be fixed through surgery. Others get meningitis. That's a painful—and serious— infection of the brain.

Valley fever is spread by breathing the spores of a fungus called *Coccidioides immitis*. It's called cocci, for short.

Cocci in the Southwest

In the southwest corner of the U.S., this fungus is a big problem.

Cocci lives in the dirt. When the soil is disturbed by anything from windstorms to dirt bikers, cocci releases poisonous spores, or seeds. The spores can cause valley fever.

Not everybody gets it. Even if the spores drift into your lungs, there's a 60 percent chance you won't get sick. And if you do, the symptoms usually range from a mild cold to painful red rashes.

There's no cure for valley fever. Experts like UCSF's Richard Hector are working on a **vaccine**. But it'll be years before they test it on humans.

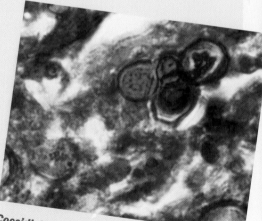

Coccidioides immitis, or "cocci," as seen through a microscope.

Demon Dust

How did this deadly fungus manage to survive in Utah?

The doctors were astonished by this diagnosis. How had the patients gotten valley fever? Valley fever is caused by a fungus called *Coccidioides immitis*, or "cocci," for short. And cocci didn't exist in northern Utah—at least until now!

To help solve this mystery, the doctors called mycologist Dr. Richard Hector. Hector works at the University of California at San Francisco.

Dr. Hector has spent his career collecting spores and analyzing mold. But mostly, he hunts cocci. This case was a real challenge. Cocci is usually found in an area called the **Lower Sonoran Life Zone**. There, cocci thrive in the dry, arid soil.

But Dinosauer National Monument is in northern Utah. That's 200 miles (322 km) north of the zone. The Utah winters are harsh. They should freeze the fungus. Even the nighttime summer temperatures are too cold for cocci. It shouldn't last a day in the Utah hills.

It was Dr. Hector's job to answer several disturbing questions. Why was cocci in the park? And where was it going next?

Dr. Richard Hector is an expert in cocci. He's found it among teen dirt bikers in Bakersfield, Arizona. He'd found it on Navy SEALS digging ditches in Coalinga, California. He'd never found it in northern Utah.

RUNAWAY COCCI

Cocci is usually found in a very particular area of the United States.

occi is dangerous. But it's not particularly hardy. It can't live just anywhere. Rain and cold kill it. And so do other, stronger fungi. Cocci needs dry soil and lots of heat. Places with little rainfall, hot summers, and moderate winters are cocci paradise.

Coccidioides immitis normally lives in a place called the Lower Sonoran Life Zone. That area stretches through parts of California, Mexico, Arizona, New Mexico, Nevada, Utah, and Texas (map area in blue).

That's why in 2001, scientists were shocked to find that cocci had moved 200 miles north to Dinosaur National Monument in Utah (marked by the "X").

X Marks the Spot
In 2001, cocci showed up in a new place

The X shows the site of the 2001 outbreak. The blue areas show where cases of cocci had most commonly been found before this outbreak.

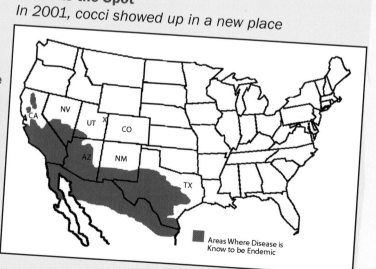

Areas Where Disease is Know to be Endemic

A Team Effort

With archeologists and geologists by his side, Dr. Hector searches for cocci's secrets.

Dr. Hector couldn't solve the mystery of the migrating cocci alone. So he put together a team of experts.

Then he and his team of scientists traveled to the dig site. They began to do some tests.

Archaeologists on Dr. Hector's team examined local ruins to understand who had lived there long ago. Was there anything in the park's past that might solve the mystery?

Geologists are experts in the earth's rocks and soils. Dr. Hector's geologists examined the area's rocks and minerals, looking for evidence that could offer new clues. They poked around in hidden caves and took samples from the nearby canyons.

Experts chip away rock around dinosaur bones at Dinosaur National Monument. It was during an expedition like this one that the archaeologists and students got sick.

The team was trying to come up with a theory for how the cocci had traveled 200 miles north to Utah. Could a wind current have carried the spores? Probably not, they decided. Such a long trip would have killed the fungus.

They were stumped.

Blast from the Past

Is the answer to the cocci puzzle thousands of years old?

Then one day the team had a breakthrough.

Archaeologists working in Dinosaur National Monument found ancient cave paintings. They also found bones from people and their dogs. They realized that thousands of years before, Native American tribes had lived in the area.

These are petroglyphs—ancient carvings—from Native Americans at Dinosaur National Monument. Had ancient people brought the fungus from other regions?

They realized that these bones could hold the answer to the mystery.

Dr. Hector and the scientists believed the tribes had moved from cocci-rich places like Arizona. Some of them—and their dogs—could have been infected with valley fever. When they were buried, their bodies would have introduced cocci into the ground, where it would have grown.

But how could cocci have survived Utah's cold temperatures?

The geologists helped answer this question. The site where the diggers had been working was under a rocky overhang. The cave-like space kept the soil dry during heavy rains. And it faced south. So it was in sunlight all year. The area was so hot that locals call it the Swelter Shelter.

The cocci case could have been a bizarre coincidence. Native Americans could have brought the fungus in their lungs from Arizona to Utah. They were buried in the Swelter Shelter. The fungus could have seeped into the soil with their bodies. And the cave's unusual location could have allowed cocci to thrive in a patch of dirt.

Case Closed?

The investigation was over—but the cocci was still on the loose.

The mystery was solved. Sort of. There was no way to *prove* that Native Americans brought cocci to Utah.

In the end, Dr. Hector's team settled for a **hypothesis**. That's an explanation based on the best observations and research—but not yet proven by facts. It's not the most satisfying conclusion to a mystery. But, as Dr. Hector says, science isn't always an exact, umm, science.

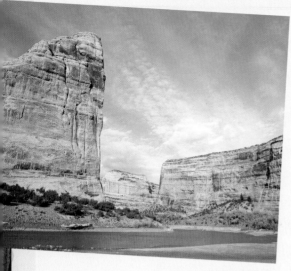

Left and below: Scenes from Dinosaur National Monument. Is there cocci lurking underground?

Now visitors to Dinosaur National Monument are warned about the areas with cocci.

Dr. Hector has gone back to his lab. He spends most of his time trying to find a vaccine for valley fever. But now and then, he can't help thinking about the case of the disease in the dirt.

"We know cocci is there. We know it's not supposed to be. And we know it can make people sick," he says. "That's the best we can do for now." **24/7**

[Fungal Fact]
During World War II (1939–1945), American troops held captured Nazi soldiers in Arizona prison camps. Some of the German prisoners became infected with valley fever from the cocci that thrived in the hot, dry soil.

What happens when a fungus moves into the woods? Have a look at the next case.

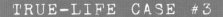
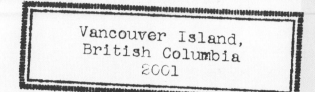

Vancouver Island,
British Columbia
2001

The Case of the Deadly Tree Fungus

How did a killer fungus travel the globe? And can a scientist find it—before it kills again?

Poison in the Air

A killer fungus is loose on a beautiful island.

In 2001, scientist Karen Bartlett got a phone call she'll never forget.

On beautiful Vancouver Island in Canada, four people had died from swelling of the brain. And 100 more had developed typical symptoms of fungal infection. They had coughs, fever, chest pains, and night sweats.

Bartlett is a professor at the University of British Columbia, Canada. She studies environmental hygiene. That means she's an expert in the **bacteria** and fungi found in homes, schools, and workplaces.

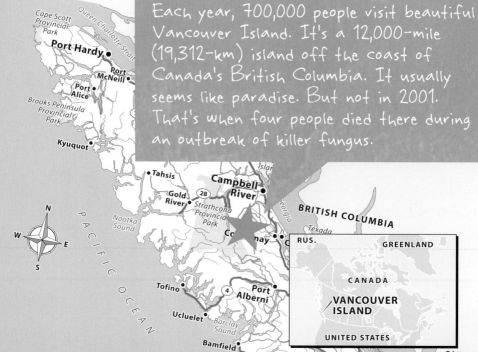

Each year, 700,000 people visit beautiful Vancouver Island. It's a 12,000-mile (19,312-km) island off the coast of Canada's British Columbia. It usually seems like paradise. But not in 2001. That's when four people died there during an outbreak of killer fungus.

"Crypto" means "secret" or "hidden." "Coccus" means "shaped like a sphere."

Or, to put it another way, she's a fungus detective.

Bartlett's first thought was that the people on Vancouver Island were the victims of cryptococcus infection. Cryptococcus—or "crypto," for short—is a deadly fungus. But it's usually found in warm, dry parts of the world like South America and Australia. It is also found in people with AIDS.

So how did it end up killing four previously healthy people in Canada?

Karen Bartlett is a professor at the University of British Columbia. She is an expert in bacteria and fungus.

On the Case!

An expert prepares to search for deadly crypto.

Bartlett immediately headed off to Vancouver Island. That's an island off the coast of Canada's British Columbia. And it's a vacation paradise. The island has tall forests, rocky seashores, and lots of wildlife wonders, from bears to porpoises.

But Bartlett wasn't taking a vacation. She was racing the clock.

Somehow, the crypto fungus had made a

home on the island. You couldn't see it. Or smell it. But it was in the trees and in the air. And if it got in your lungs, it could be deadly.

Each year, 700,000 tourists visit Vancouver Island. Were they bringing cryptococcus home with them as souvenirs? Could Bartlett stop the fungus before it spread to the rest of Canada—and beyond?

"People think of scientists as living in this ivory tower where we do research and look into microscopes all day," she says. "But some of the great adventures are found outside the lab."

Bartlett's great adventure was about to begin.

Scientists like Karen Bartlett study molds and other organisms in petri dishes like this one. But they also make important discoveries in the field.

WHAT IS CRYPTOCOCCUS?

It lives in trees and likes warm places. And if you inhale it, you could die!

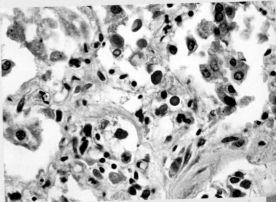

Cryptococcus, as seen through a microscope.

You probably don't think of yeast as a killer.

But there is one very dangerous kind of yeast: cryptococcus—or crypto, for short. Crypto lives in trees. Its favorite spot is eucalyptus trees. It usually thrives in warm, dry places like Brazil and Australia.

Crypto Spores

The trouble starts when cryptococcus gives off spores—and people or animals breathe them in. You can't see the spores. Or smell them. But when they get into your lungs, they can cause a yellowy fungus that scientists can view under a microscope.

Cryptococcus infection is extremely rare. Fewer than one or two people per million get it each year. But if you get it, the symptoms can be bad.

Mild cases cause coughs, fever, chest pains, and night sweats. But in severe cases, patients can need lung surgery—or may even die from swelling of the brain.

[Fungal Fact]

Fungi are hungry creatures. But they don't have mouths and stomachs. Instead, they absorb food with their outer surfaces as they grow. When they get hungry, they simply expand outward, absorbing all the organisms they touch.

The Search

Bartlett tracks the killer fungus on Vancouver Island.

THE QUESTION Bartlett had two mysteries to solve: Where exactly was cryptococcus hiding? And how did it manage to survive on cool, damp Vancouver Island?

A field worker removes loose tree bark to search for fungi. Bartlett had to examine trees all over the island to find the crypto.

Bartlett knew the fungus lived in trees. Now she had to find the right ones. That wouldn't be easy. There are trees everywhere on Vancouver Island—eucalyptus, Douglas firs, big-leaf maples.

THE EVIDENCE Bartlett would have to examine all the trees until she found the fungus.

She crisscrossed the island, searching the vast forests. She tiptoed into backyards, breaking off bits of bark. She swabbed sap with a Q-tip. And she took air samples with a pump that works like a vacuum cleaner.

Bartlett brought her mountain of samples back to the lab. For weeks, she pored over drips of sap and specks of dirt.

Finally, she found her fungus!

THE CONCLUSION Only one small sampling tested positive for crypto. The fungus was nestled in a batch of trees along the island's east coast.

The first mystery was solved!

Second Mystery Solved

Bartlett found her killer fungus. But how had it managed to survive?

Bartlett found the small batch of trees where the crypto lived. The fungus isn't supposed to survive in cool, wet environments like Vancouver Island. What was keeping it alive?

All of the crypto-infected trees were in an east coast strip of "rain shadow." This piece of land sits in the shadow of Washington's Olympic Mountains. The mountains block the rain clouds, leaving a stretch of island that is unusually warm and dry. Those are the exact conditions cryptococcus likes.

Crypto may have lived in the rain shadow for five years—or 500. No one knows.

But one thing was certain: Cryptococcus didn't act up until a few years before. Why? Bartlett thought that cryptococcus could have had some help from **global warming**.

Vancouver Island's weather was changing. Not by much. In fact, the temperature had shifted just a fraction of a degree in 20 years. But that was enough to make the summers slightly drier and the winters just a bit warmer. That tiny change could have warmed cryptococcus and caused it to release its killer spores.

The Douglas firs on Vancouver Island usually provide a lot of cool shade. And that's not an environment in which crypto usually thrives.

Still on the Loose

Bartlett tracked the fungus to its source. But that doesn't mean she can keep it from killing again.

There was one more twist. Bartlett had found the cryptococcus—but she couldn't get rid of it.

Many fungi are treated with **fungicides**, chemicals that kill them. But crypto isn't hurt by fungicides. Cutting down the trees wouldn't work either. The spores almost certainly had taken root in the soil.

Today, tourists still flock to Vancouver Island to camp and fish. And, for the most part, cryptococcus leaves them alone. About 25 islanders become sick—and one dies—from crypto every year.

Bartlett thinks that's the best that can be done—for now. "The world is big enough for people and fungi to get along," she says. 24/7

In spite of the threat from crypto, vacationers still come to Vancouver Island to camp and enjoy the outdoors.

MEDICAL DOWNLOAD

Here's more information about the fungus among us.

IN THIS SECTION:

- ▶ amazing fungi-related discoveries from the past;
- ▶ how fungus fighters have been in the news;
- ▶ the tools that are used to study fungi;
- ▶ and is being a fungus hunter in your future?

1840s Potato Bugged
A fungus attacks Ireland. It kills so many potato plants that a million people die of hunger. It's known as the Irish Potato Famine.

1892 Down in the Valley
An Argentine soldier becomes the first person on record to contract valley fever. Doctors first tell him the sore on his cheek is a spider bite. Later, they diagnose him with cancer. Finally, they realize he has a new disease.

Key Dates in the History of Fungi

Here's the good, the bad, and the ugly about fungi.

1944 Black Death
A major outbreak of hemorrhagic disease—bleeding of the lungs—erupts in Siberia. One million die. The cause? The people were starving and ate grain infected with black fungus.

1928 Alexander the Great

Scottish researcher Alexander Fleming (*right*) accidentally discovers **penicillin**. It's a wonder drug made from a fungus that has saved millions of lives by curing nasty infections.

1930 Valley Fever

Valley fever gets its name. Of the 286 known cases, more than 90 percent are in California. Two-thirds are near the San Joaquin Valley. The disease is named for that valley.

1939 Russian Invasion

Russian dictator Josef Stalin (*right*) gets mad when his army's horses mysteriously die, hurting the military strength of his country. Veterinarians try to explain that the horses were killed by a fungus—probably stachybotrys. But Stalin suspects foul play—and executes the vets.

1969 Biology Test

Forget "animal," "vegetable," or "mineral." American biologist R. H. Whittaker discovers that fungi are so different from other organisms that they need their own classification. They are the only things on earth that don't fit into one of those three categories.

1980 Toxic Wheat

Greek farm children sleeping near a grain storage area suffer from bleeding lungs. The culprit was first thought to be a **pesticide**. Now researchers believe the grain was contaminated by toxic mold.

In the News

Read all about it! Fungi are front-page news.

Fungus May Help Cure Malaria!

EDINBURGH, SCOTLAND—June 10, 2005

Scientists say a fungus that's harmless to humans may be used to kill the mosquitoes that cause **malaria**. Malaria kills more than one million people a year in Africa and elsewhere. It especially attacks children under five years old.

In their study, scientists from Scotland sprayed the fungus *Beauveria bassiana* into cardboard traps where mosquitoes lived. Many of the insects died within 14 days. Others grew sick and couldn't fly.

The fungus can't hurt people, though. That's because human bodies are too warm for it to grow.

A research assistant examines a fungus culture in a petri dish. Scientists are studying the fungus *Beauveria bassiana* to find out if it could kill mosquitoes infected with the parasite that causes malaria.

A homeowner in New Orleans removes a mirror from mold-covered walls. Her house was flooded during Hurricane Katrina, and a dangerous mold grew on the walls.

Mold Attacks New Orleans After Hurricane Katrina!

Mold creates patterns on the walls and ceiling of another flood-damaged house in New Orleans.

NEW ORLEANS, LA—October 2005

Hurricane Katrina struck New Orleans and nearby cities in August 2005. The storm caused massive flooding—which resulted in the growth of mold. Scientists say that nearly half the houses in the affected area had mold. And the people who lived there were at risk for lung disease—and worse.

To keep people from getting sick, experts had to destroy the mold. In some cases, they brought in big air conditioners that killed the mold with cold air. In others, they turned on furnaces that killed the mold with heat. When the mold was too bad, the houses had to be torn down. "We've had floods before," said one expert. "But nothing like this!"

The Fungus Among Us

Have a look at some of the equipment used by mycologists and other scientists.

microscope Many fungi are so tiny you can't see them. A microscope is a scientific tool with a special lens that makes everything look much bigger. By viewing a fungus sample with a high-tech "super" microscope, scientists can see it and figure out what type it is.

Q-tips You might use Q-tips on your ears. Mycologists use them to collect samples of fungi that live in sticky sap from trees.

X-acto knife Experts use an X-acto knife to cut away mold from walls and other places. Then they use bleach to clean the surface.

tape tape is the easiest way for an environmental hygienist to collect a sample of mold from a house's walls or pipes.

auger An auger is a long pipe that scientists drill into the ground to collect samples of soil containing fungi.

suma canister This device is used to collect air samples. These air samples are then examined for the presence of fungi and spores.

goggles Scientists wear goggles to keep fungi spores from getting into their eyes.

N-95 respirator mask Mycologists wear an N-95 respirator mask over their nose and mouth to keep tiny fungi spores from getting into their lungs.

fungicide Fungicide is a chemical that kills fungi. But some fungi aren't hurt by fungicide and must be removed by hand.

PENICILLIN: THE WORLD'S MOST FAMOUS FUNGUS

One accident saved millions of lives.

Some fungi are killers. But one special fungus has saved millions of lives.

If you were living before 1928 and you got a serious infection—anything from pneumonia to a bullet wound—your chances of survival weren't very good. Tiny organisms called bacteria caused these bad infections. And doctors couldn't cure them.

That is until a Scottish researcher named Alexander Fleming made an accidental discovery.

Fleming had seen the horrors of infection during World War I (1914–1918). Without proper treatment, even small battlefield wounds killed many soldiers. Fleming worked for years to find a medicine that stopped bacteria. But he had no success. He grew sample bacteria in small plates called petri dishes as he searched for an answer.

TAKE A LOOK AT HOW PENICILLIN GOES TO WORK ON BACTERIA.

Here's penicillin in action. The white stuff taking up most of the left side of the petri dish is staph bacteria. The little white dot in the center of the staph is penicillin. You can see how the penicillin has killed the staph bacteria immediately around it.

PENICILLIUM MOULD

FROM PROFESSOR ALEXANDER FLEMING 1935

This penicillin mold belonged to Alexander Fleming. It was sold for $25,000 in 1997.

Night Mold

One night in 1928, Fleming left his bacteria-filled petri dishes uncovered near an open window. Days later, he found odd, empty circles in his dishes. To Fleming's surprise, a stray fungus had blown through the window and killed the bacteria.

The fungus was called *Penicillium notatum*, and it was related to ordinary bread mold. It would be used to make penicillin—the first **antibiotic**—and would save millions of lives!

HELP WANTED:
Mycologist

Are you a future fungus hunter? Here's more information about the field.

Q&A: DR. RICHARD HECTOR

24/7: Tell us about your job.

DR. RICHARD HECTOR: I'm a microbiologist. That's a scientist who studies microbes—living organisms that are too small for the eye to see. There are many different species of microbes: bacteria, protozoa, viruses, and fungi. I specialize in fungi.

24/7: So you're also a mycologist?

DR. HECTOR: Yes, I'm a medical mycologist. That means I study the fungi that cause diseases. I became interested in the field by studying valley fever.

24/7: What does a mycologist do?

DR. HECTOR: My specialty is cocci. So I spend a lot of time testing the fungus to learn how it spreads valley fever. The more I know about it, the more I can predict how it will act. One day I might learn enough to create a vaccine to fight it.

24/7: How do you test fungi?

DR. HECTOR: First, I try to get samples of the fungus. That's to learn what type we're dealing with and where it's hiding. In the case of cocci, I drill augers—long pipes—into the soil. The pipes suck up enough dirt for me to study under a microscope.

51

24/7: Why is it hard to find the fungus?

DR. HECTOR: They are microscopic needles in a haystack. First, you have to find the right patch of dirt to dig. Sometimes we're working in miles of dirt. Then you have to dig at the right depth.

The temperature on the day you dig may ruin all your work. A humid day may drown your samples. A chilly day could freeze them. It's rare that we actually find cocci.

24/7: Is it hard to do all that work and never see the fungus?

DR. HECTOR: You don't always need to see the fungus to know it's there. Let me tell you a true story that shows what I mean.

A group of scientists visited the Mojave Desert to get a cocci sample. They drove up and down dirt roads in areas they thought held the fungus. They collected tons of dust. And they couldn't find cocci in one speck of it. But everyone on the truck caught valley fever!

If you're a scientist, sometimes you have to be satisfied with an incomplete answer.

Dr. Richard Hector is a mycologist at the University of California at San Francisco.

I'M NOT SMART ENOUGH TO BE A SCIENTIST (AND OTHER MYTHS)

I don't want to go to school forever. I'll spend my life in the lab. Excuses, excuses. Here's the truth about careers in science.

MYTH: I'm not smart enough to be a scientist.

TRUTH: Scientists aren't any more or less intelligent than anyone else. But instead of studying law or business, they study science. Being a good scientist has more to do with curiosity and dedication than with brains.

MYTH: Scientists have to go to school forever!

TRUTH: True, most scientists have degrees beyond a high school diploma and a four-year college bachelor of science. If you go for the highest degree, a PhD, then you may spend nine years in college—or more.

But you don't have to wait that long to start working. You can put your scientific skills to use while getting those degrees.

MYTH: I'd have to spend all day in the lab. Boring!

TRUTH: You can't avoid spending some time peering into microscopes. But that's not the only part of a scientist's job.

Mycologists go where the fungi are—and that's everywhere on earth. One day you're hiking through the Mojave Desert. The next month you're trekking through the Amazon rain forest. Maybe you're even standing on the edge of an active volcano!

MYTH: How can I find out if I should pursue a career in science?

TRUTH: Just asking questions shows that you may have science in your future. Talk to your science teachers about their careers. Look for science adventures in the library and on the Web. Visit a science museum. Get involved with your school's science club or science fairs.

In high school, take biology, chemistry, physics, computer science, and math. And don't forget English classes. Scientists do a lot of writing. Even foreign languages can help you. Scientists share information around the world.

Take this totally unscientific quiz to see if fungus-fighting might be a good career for you.

1 What's your feeling about science class?
a) I stay after school to look at microscope slides.
b) I'm doing okay, but I'd rather be at lunch.
c) I wouldn't know. I sleep through it.

2 Can you handle lots of homework?
a) Bring it on.
b) It piles up, but I always finish it.
c) I think I left it in my locker. Or on the bus. Or under my bed.

3 Are you easily grossed out?
a) The slimier the fungus, the better.
b) I can stomach it.
c) Yuck! Get it off! Get it off!

4 How do you feel about the great outdoors?
a) Love it! The more I can be in nature, the better.
b) I spend time outside. But I wouldn't want to live there.
c) Where do I plug in my PS2?

5 Are you curious about things?
a) I want to know who, what, where, why, and how.
b) Depends on the subject. I'm either very interested—or I don't care at all.
c) What did you say? I wasn't listening.

YOUR SCORE

Give yourself 3 points for every "a" you chose. Give yourself 2 points for every "b" you chose. Give yourself 1 point for every "c" you chose.

If you got **13–15** points, you're a born fungus fighter!

If you got **10–12** points, you might make a good mycologist.

If you got **5–9** points, you might want to look for another career!

HOW TO GET STARTED... NOW!

It's never too early to start working toward your goals.

GET AN EDUCATION

▶ Starting now, take as many biology, chemistry, physics, computer science, English, and math courses as you can. Train yourself to ask questions, gather new information, and make conclusions the way mycologists do.

▶ Read any books and magazine articles you can find about fungi.

▶ Read the newspaper and visit science Web sites. Keep up with the latest news about fungi.

▶ Graduate from high school. Get good grades!

▶ Research colleges now. Look for ones with good science programs. Call or write to those colleges to get information.

NETWORK!

Ask your own doctor, school guidance counselor, or science teacher for advice about becoming a mycologist. See if you can find a local scientist who might be willing to give you advice. Maybe you can spend a day with him or her to see what the job is like.

GET AN INTERNSHIP

▶ Look for an internship with a mycologist or other scientist.

▶ Begin by contacting the nearest college or university. It never hurts to ask if they need interns.

READ ANYTHING YOU CAN FIND ABOUT FUNGI.

See the books and Web sites in the Resources section beginning on page 56.

LEARN ABOUT OTHER JOBS IN THE FIELD

Mycologists are experts in fungus. But other scientists also work with fungi including: environmental hygienists, biologists, infectious disease specialists, geologists, and doctors—to name just a few.

Resources

Looking for more information? Here are some resources you don't want to miss!

SCHOOLS

Cornell University
www.human.cornell.edu
School of Human Ecology
170 Martha Van Rensselaer Hall
Ithaca, NY 14853-4401
PHONE: 607-255-5471
E-MAIL: humec_admissions
@cornell.edu

Duke University
www.biology.duke.edu
Office of Undergraduate
Studies, Department of Biology
Room 135
Biological Sciences Building
Box 90338
Durham, NC 27708-0338
PHONE: 919-660-7372
E-MAIL: biodus@duke.edu

**University of
British Columbia**
www.ubc.ca
2329 West Mall Vancouver, BC
Canada V6T 1Z4
PHONE: 604-822-2211
E-MAIL: international.
reception@ubc.ca

**University of
California, Berkeley**
www.berkeley.edu
College of Natural Resources
Student Resource Center
260 Mulford Hall
Berkeley, CA 94720-3114
PHONE: 510-642-7171
E-MAIL: cnrmain@nature.
berkeley.edu

University of Texas at Austin
www.utexas.edu
Office of Admissions
P.O. Box 8058
Austin, TX 78713-8058
PHONE: 512-475-7399

University of Toronto
www.utoronto.ca
25 Kings College Circle
Toronto, Ontario, Canada M5S 1A1
PHONE: 416-978-5000
E-MAIL: information.commons
@utoronto.ca

PROFESSIONAL ORGANIZATIONS

American Phytopathological Society (APS)

www.apsnet.org
3340 Pilot Knob Road
St. Paul, MN 55121
PHONE: (651) 454-7250
E-MAIL: aps@scisoc.org

The APS is an international scientific organization devoted to the study of plant diseases and their control.

Centers for Disease Control and Prevention (CDC)

www.msaf
1600 Clifton Road
Atlanta, GA 30333
PHONE: 800-311-3435

The CDC was founded in 1946, primarily to fight malaria. It is part of the Department of Health and Human Services. Today, the group is a leader in efforts to prevent and control disease, injuries, workplace hazards, and environmental and health threats.

Mycological Society of America (MSA)

www.msafungi.org
P.O. Box 7065
Lawrence, KS 66044
PHONE: 800-627-0629

This is a scientific society dedicated to advancing the study of fungi of all kinds, including mushrooms, molds, truffles, yeasts, lichens, plant pathogens, and medically important fungi.

National Institute of Allergy and Infectious Disease (NIAID)

www3.niaid.nih.gov/
6610 Rockledge Drive, MSC 612
Bethesda, MD 20892
PHONE: 301-496-5717

For more than 50 years, NIAID has conducted research that helps treat, prevent, and better understand infectious and other diseases. It is part of the National Institutes of Health.

WEB SITES

Bell Museum of Natural History

www.bellmuseum.org

This Minneapolis museum has one of the world's best fungal collections.

Doctor Fungus

www.doctorfungus.org

Learn about fungal diseases and see stachy, crypto, and a host of other fungi on this site.

The Hidden Forest

www.hiddenforest.co.nz

Take a virtual trip inside a New Zealand forest, and discover such treats as dung fungi and slime molds.

Introduction to the Fungi
www.ucmp.berkeley.edu/fungi/
fungi.html

Learn some fun fungal facts,
from this University of California,
Berkeley site

Mycological Institute for the Study of Fungal Mold in Human Habitations
www.njmoldinspection.com/what_
is_mycology.html

Learn about careers in fungi and all
about mycology and fungi.

Mycology Online
www.mycology.adelaide.edu.au/
Fungal_Jungle

Want to explore a fungal jungle?
This site from the University of
Adelaide in Australia has pictures
and descriptions of all the fungus
among us.

MykoWeb
www.mykoweb.com

This fun site is devoted to the
science of mycology. It includes
everything from funky fungal
pictures to mushroom recipes.

WWW Virtual Library: Mycology
mycology.cornell.edu/

Everything you'd ever want to
know about fungi—as told by
Cornell University scientists.

BOOKS

Birch, Beverly. *Alexander Fleming* (Giants of Science). San Diego:
Blackbirch Press, 2002.

Pasoe, Elaine. *Slime, Mold and Fungi* (Nature Up-Close). San Diego:
Blackbirch Press, 1998.

Silverman, Buffy. *Molds and Fungi* (The KidHaven Science Library).
San Diego: KidHaven, 2004.

Snedden, Robert. *Plants and Fungi: Multicelled Life* (Cells and
Life). Portsmouth, N.H.: Heinemann, 2002.

Souza, Dorothy M. *What Is a Fungus?* (Watts Library). Danbury,
Conn.: Franklin Watts, 2002.

Viegas, Jennifer. *Fungi and Molds* (Germs! The Library of
Disease-Causing Organisms). New York: Rosen Publishing, 2004.

A

allergies (AH-ler-jeez) *noun* physical reactions to certain substances; these include sneezing, having trouble breathing, and itching

allergists (AH-ler-jists) *noun* scientists who study the causes of allergies and treat people who have them

antibiotic (an-tee-bye-OH-tik) *noun* a substance that fights bacteria; doctors prescribe antibiotics to patients with infections

archaeologists (ar-kee-OL-uh-jists) *noun* scientists who learn about the past by digging up old buildings and objects and studying them

auger (OH-ger) *noun* a long pipe that is drilled into the ground; scientists use augers to collect samples of fungi

B

bacteria (bak-TEAR-ee-uh) *noun* a microscopic one-celled organism; some bacteria are essential for our survival and others may cause disease

biologists (bye-OL-uh-jists) *noun* scientists who study living organisms

C

CDC (see-dee-SEE) *noun* a government agency in charge of protecting public health. It is short for the *Centers for Disease Control and Prevention*.

Coccidioides immitis (KOK-sih-dee-OY-des ih-MYTE-is) *noun* a fungus that usually lives in the soil in certain parts of the southwestern United States and northern Mexico. When the dirt is unsettled, it releases dangerous spores that can spark a disease called valley fever. It is sometimes called cocci for short.

contagious (kuhn-TAY-juhss) *adjective* describing something, like an illness, that can be spread from person to person by contact

cryptococcus (krip-tuh-KOK-us) *noun* a type of fungus usually found in soil or on trees. In rare cases, it can cause an infection when inhaled. It is often called crypto for short.

E

environmental hygienists (en-VYE-ro-men-tal HYE-jeh-nists) *noun* scientists who study fungi and other organisms found in human environments, like homes, schools, and workplaces

F

fungicides (FUHN-jih-sidez) *noun* chemicals that kill fungi

fungus (FUHN-guhss) *noun* a member of a group of organisms that belong to their own species kingdom; the plural is fungi. Fungi include molds, mildews, yeasts, mushrooms, and puffballs.

G

geologists (jee-OL-uh-jists) *noun* scientists who study the earth's rocks and minerals

global warming (GLO-buhl WAR-ming) *noun* a gradual warming of the earth's atmosphere, thought to be caused primarily by pollutants

H

hypothesis (hye-PAH-thuh-sis) *noun* an idea based on evidence that is not complete; an educated guess

I

infectious disease specialists (in-FEK-shuhss duh-ZEEZ SPESH-uh-lists) *noun* researchers who work with blood samples and x-rays to figure out how to treat complicated illnesses

L

Lower Sonoran Life Zone (LOW-er suh-NOR-uhn life zone) *noun* the parts of the American Southwest and parts of Mexico where the cocci fungus is known to grow. It stretches through parts of California and Mexico into Arizona, New Mexico, and Texas.

M

malaria (mah-LAR-ee-ah) *noun* a serious infection transmitted by a mosquito bite

meningitis (men-in-JYE-tis) *noun* an infection of the lining of the brain

mildews (MIL-doos) *noun* fungal substances that grow on organic matter and other surfaces; you might see some mildew in a dirty shower stall

mold (mold) *noun* a dangerous type of fungus that can produce allergy-like symptoms. Some molds grow on old cheese. Exposure to certain kinds of mold can be fatal.

mycologist (mye-KOL-uh-jist) *noun* a scientist who studies fungi

mycotoxin (mye-koh-TOK-sin) *noun* a poison produced by the spores from some mold

O

outbreaks (OUT-brakes) *noun* sudden spreading of disease in a short period of time and in a limited geographic location (like a neighborhood, community, school, or hospital)

P

penicillin (peh-nih-SIL-un) *noun* an antibiotic drug, made from a fungus and used to treat infection

pesticide (PESS-tuh-side) *noun* a chemical used to kill pests, such as insects

prognosis (prog-NOH-suhss) *noun* a prediction of what an illness is expected to do in the future

pulmonary hemosiderosis (PUL-muh-nar-ee hee-mo-sid-ur-OH-sis) *noun* a medical condition where the lungs fill with blood

S

spores (sporz) *noun* the seeds of mold or fungi; breathing them can be dangerous

stachybotrys (stak-ee-BUI-ruhs) *noun* a dangerous mold that produces toxic spores. Also known as toxic mold or black mold and called stachy for short.

symptoms (SIMP-tuhmz) *noun* the noticeable signs of a disease

T

thrive (thrive) *verb* to do well and flourish

toxic (TOK-sik) *adjective* poisonous

V

vaccine (VAK-seen) *noun* a medicine that prevents a disease

valley fever (VAL-ee FEE-vur) *noun* a fungal disease contracted by inhaling dust particles that have spores of the fungus *Coccidioides immitis*, or cocci. Most cases produce mild allergy-like symptoms. Serious cases can be life-threatening.

Y

yeasts (yeests) *noun* types of fungi that help bread to rise but can also cause disease

Index

Author's Note

I'll be honest. I was never much of a fungus fan. Sure, I like mushrooms in my salad. And there would be no bread without yeast. But when I think fungus, I picture athlete's foot, ringworm, and belly button lint. Yuck!

I can't say writing this book changed my mind about fungi. I still think they're pretty gross. In fact, the fungi I researched for this book—stachy, cocci, and crypto—do a lot worse than cause dry skin and itchy toes. They can kill you.

Writing this book hasn't made me love fungi. But it's made me think twice about the people who hunt the deadly types. It's not a glamorous job. But they do it for one reason. Well, two really. They are scientists who devote their lives to studying new organisms wherever they find them. And they want to keep the rest of us safe.

While writing this book, I visited libraries and Web sites. I read many books and articles. But I found that the best way to get good information was to go right to the source. No, not the fungi. The scientists.

A lot of dedicated mycologists, geologists, and environmental hygienists spent hours talking to me about how they do their work. Without their help, this book wouldn't be possible. And without their hard work, well, I know I'd think twice before ordering mushrooms on my pizza.

CONTENT ADVISER: Mark S. Dworkin, MD, MPH & TM, Associate Professor, Division of Epidemiology and Biostatistics, University of Illinois at Chicago

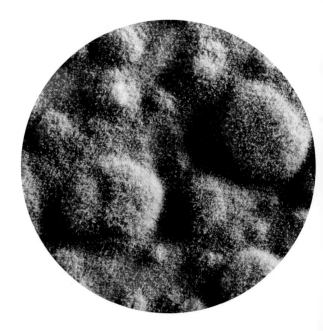